I0484962

I'm A Artist

Will You Draw With Me?

Written By
Bailey de Cardenas

April de Cardenas

Hand Drawn Artwork
Bailey de Cardenas
Age 5

ISBN
ISBN is 1449954324 and EAN-13 is 9781449954321.

Printed In The United States Of America

"Get Ready, Grab Your Crayons, Let's Go Draw!"

Bailey de Cardenas

I'm A Artist!

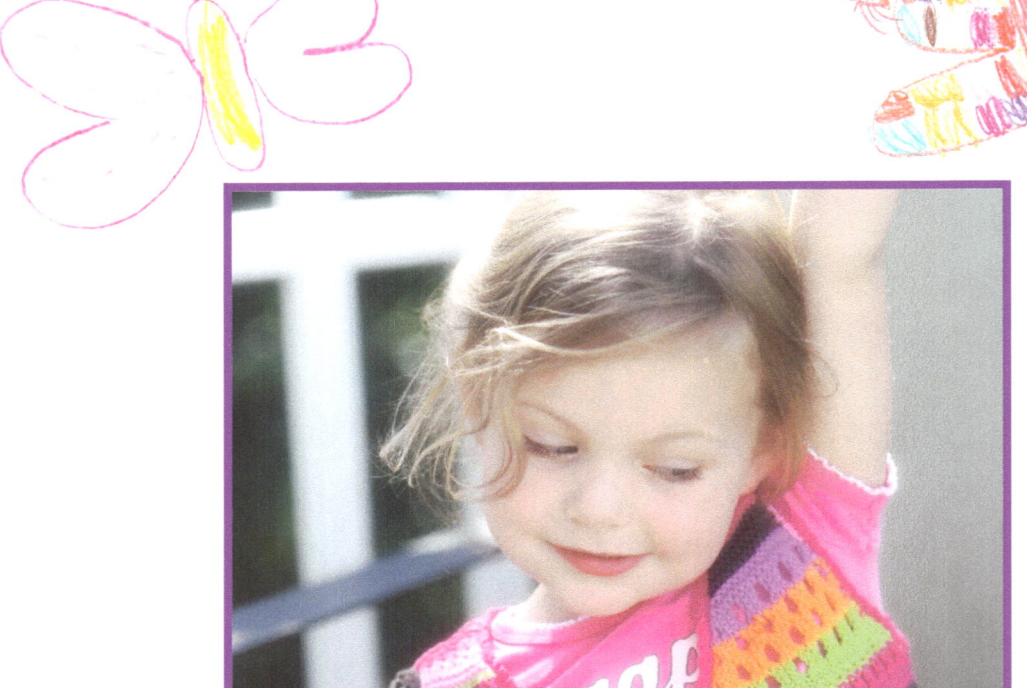

Will You Draw With Me?

About Me!

My Name Is: **BAiLeY**

I Am **5** Years Old.

I Am in **kindergarten** In School.

I Have **3** Brothers and **2** Sisters.

My Favorite Color is **Pink**

I Have **Deer** For A Pet, They Live In My **Yard**

My Favorite Thing To Do Is **Draw**

My Favorite Holiday Is **X-mas**

When I Grow Up I Want To Be A **Artist**

I Like Me Because **I'm special**

My Favorite Animal Is A **Cat**

My Favorite Food Is **Taco's**

My Favorite Toy Is A **Doll**

About You!

My Name Is:_____.

I Am _____ Years Old.

I Am in _____ In School.

I Have _____ Brothers and _____ Sisters.

My Favorite Color is _____.

I Have _____ For A Pet, They Live In My _____.

My Favorite Thing To Do Is _____.

My Favorite Holiday Is _____.

When I Grow Up I Want To Be A _____

I Like Me Because _____.

My Favorite Animal Is A _____.

My Favorite Food Is _____.

My Favorite Toy Is A
_____.

I LIKE YOU!

I like to draw and paint. My mommy is an artist and writer, I want to be just like her. I made this book so you could have fun with me drawing and using our imaginations. Would you like that? GREAT!

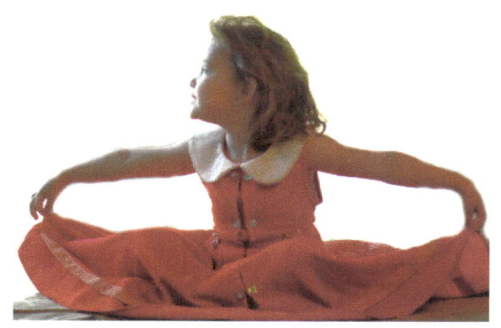

Here is a picture of a cat I drew, would you like to color it for me? Terrific!

Color Me!

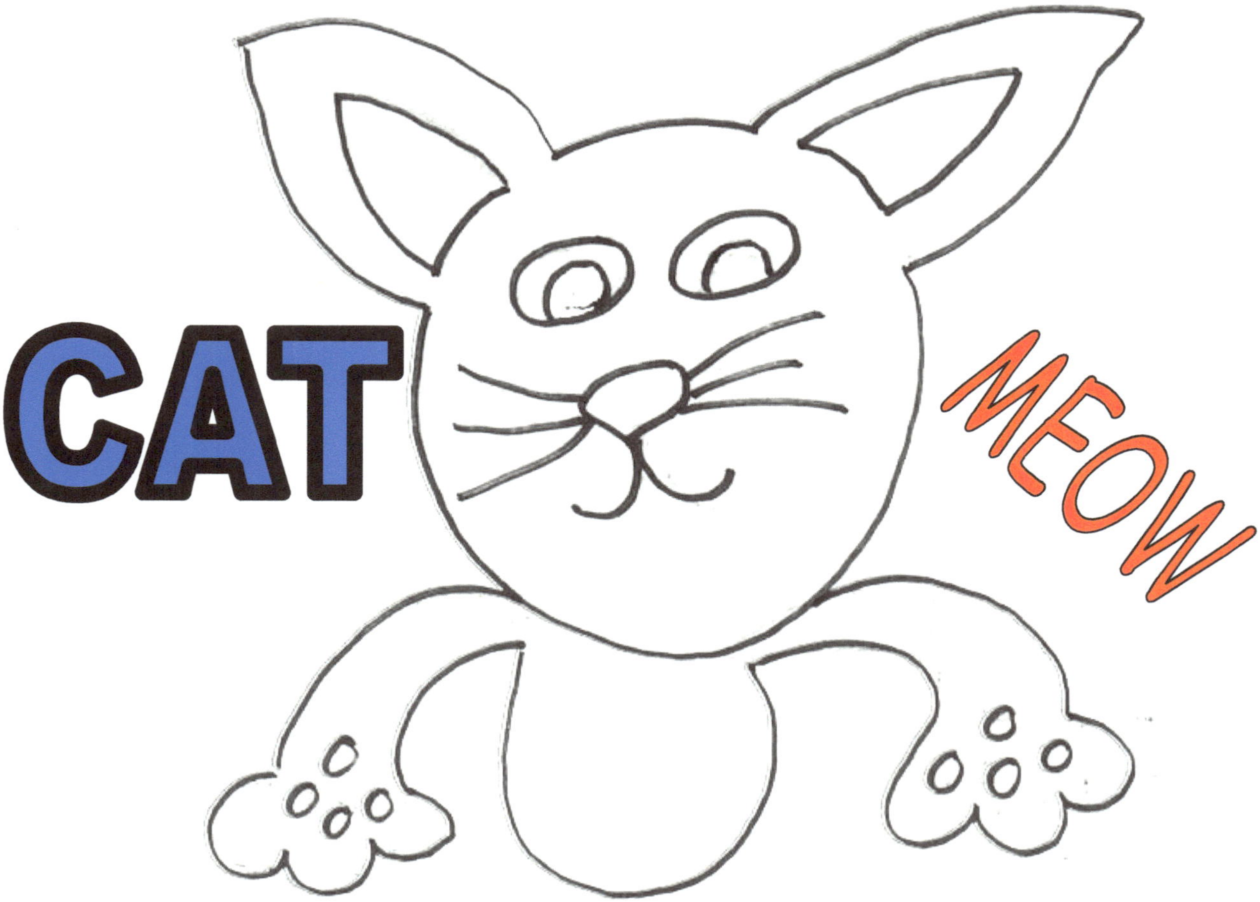

CAT

MEOW

CAN YOU DRAW A CAT?

I like bunnies also. I have lots of them in my yard. They hop really high in the air. Sometimes, I catch the bunnies playing with each other. The bunny rabbits look like they are playing chase! I have tried to catch one but they are very fast. I bet that they are soft. Can you color my bunny? Yippee!

Hop

Hop

BUNNY

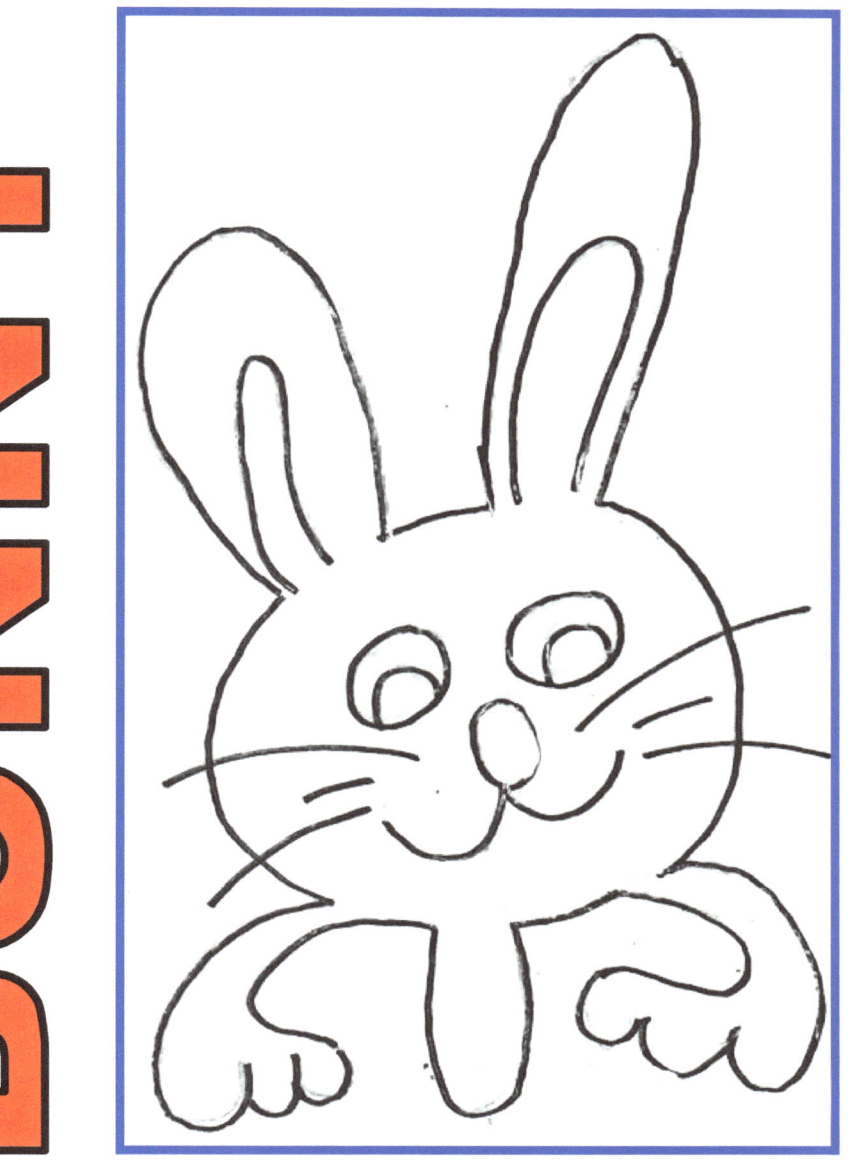

CAN YOU DRAW A BUNNY?

My neighbor has a dog. Sometimes, I see the dog looking out his window at me. He is really cute. I play outside with him. He likes to play catch with a ball.

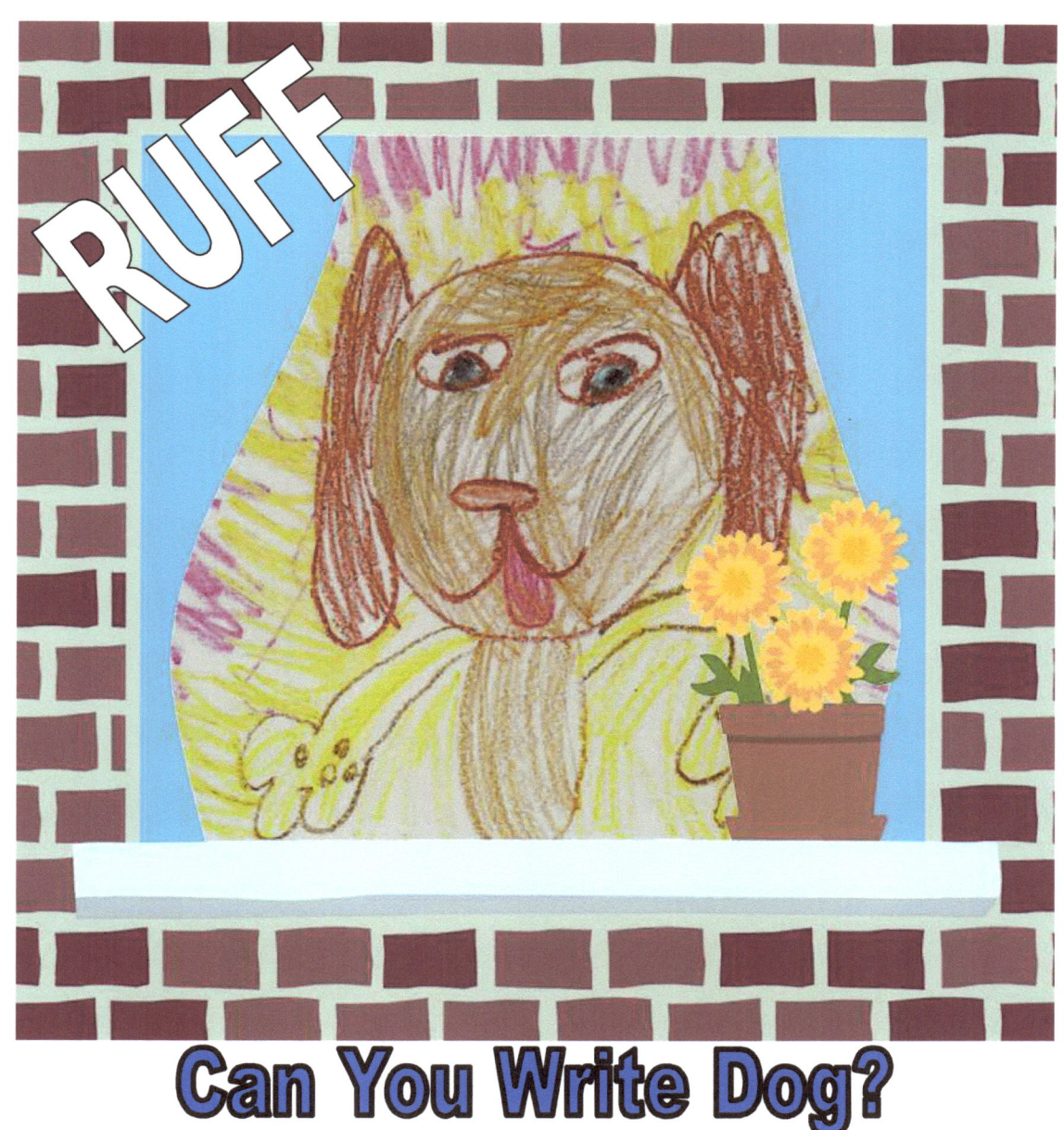

Can You Write Dog?

_____

CAN YOU DRAW A DOG?

My teacher taught me that I could use my hand to make a turkey. It was so easy! Do you like my drawing?

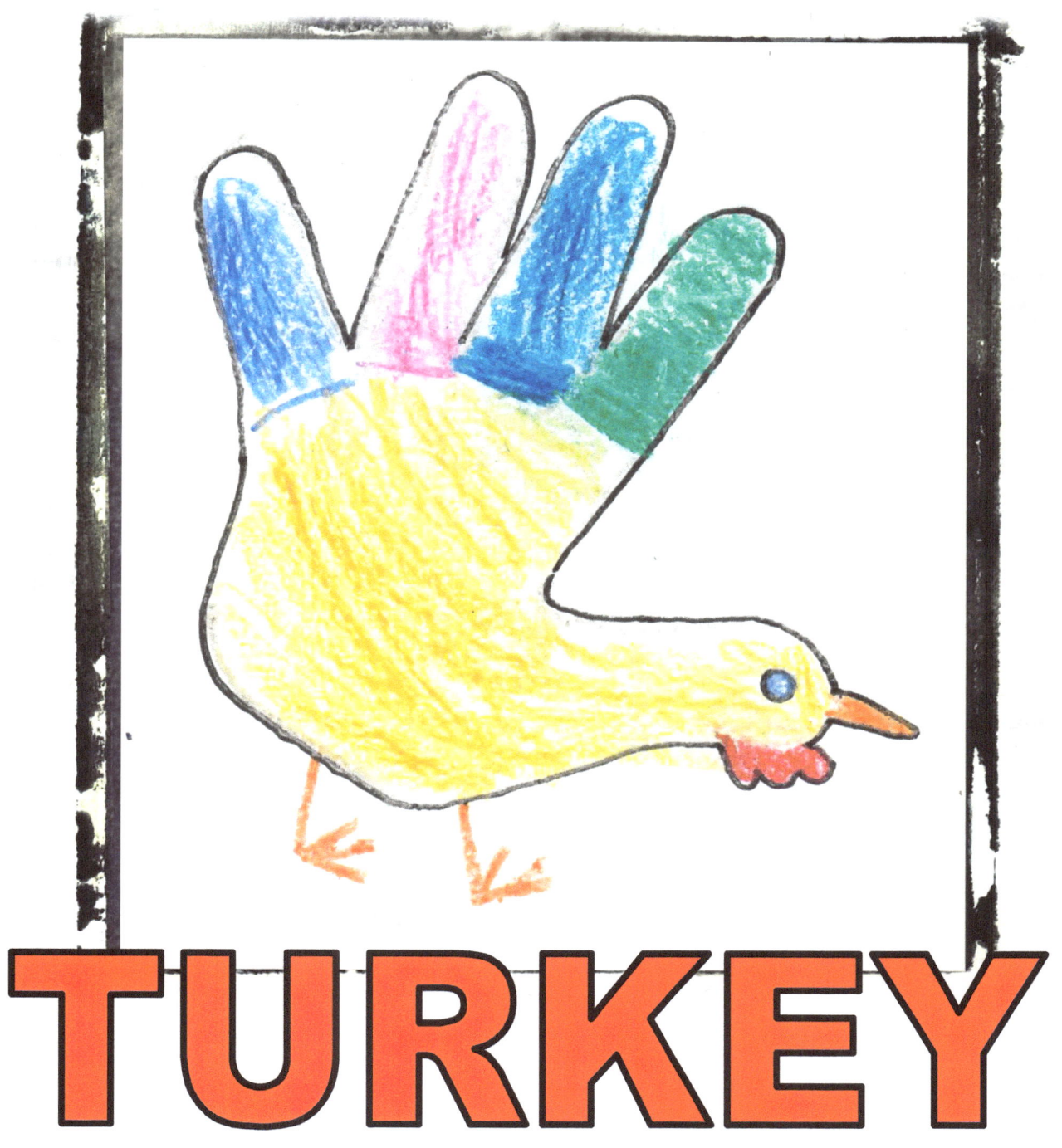

TURKEY

CAN YOU DRAW A TURKEY?

I LOVE CHRISTMAS!

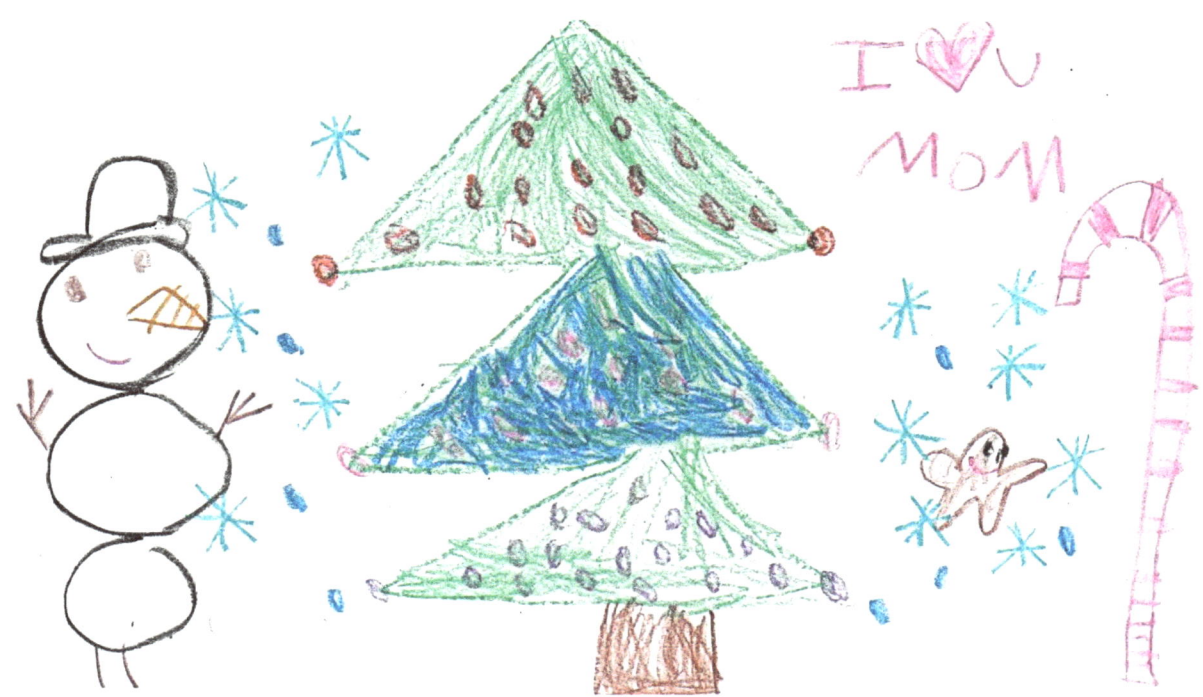

CANDY CANE

I love Christmas! I love the decorations and parties at school. I love winter time and playing in the snow. Of course, I love the presents also. I try really hard to be good for Santa all year. Can you be good with me?

I wish you lived near me, then we could make snow angels together.

CAN YOU DRAW A SNOW MAN?

I like to design things. You can never draw something wrong because everyone see's art different with their own eyes. I drew this design of flowers and a rainbow together. Do you like my design?

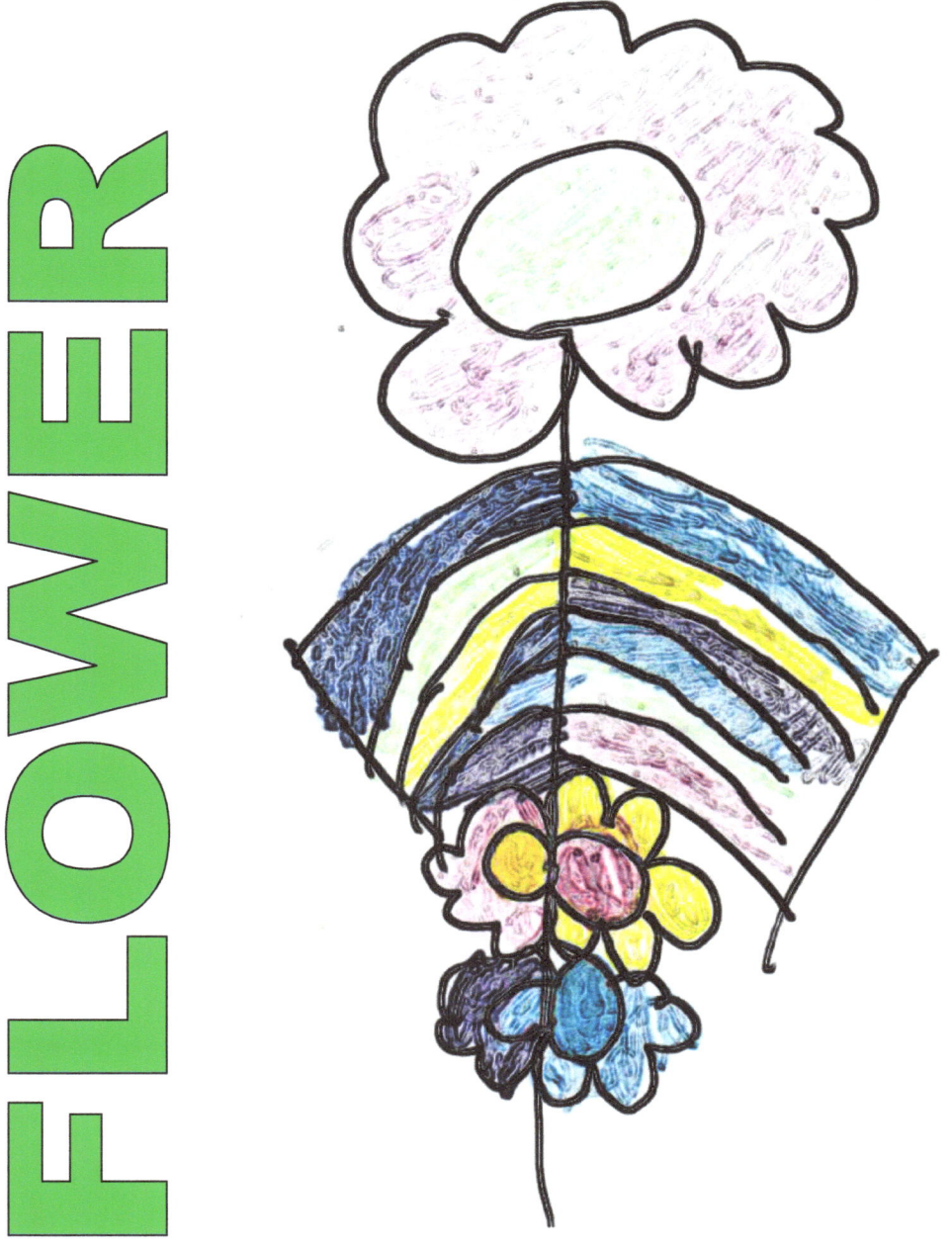

FLOWER

Make A Design Here.‒

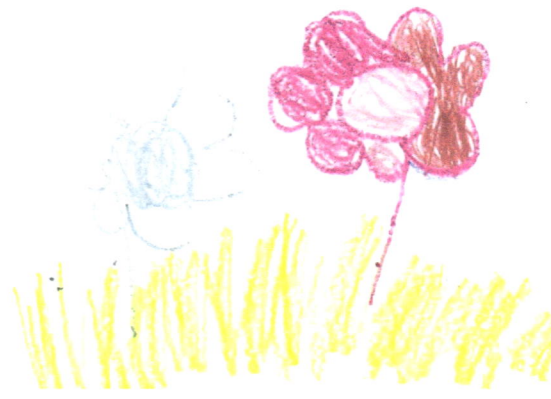

Beautiful!

YUMMY!

I Love Cupcakes and Cooking!

Sometimes my Mommy let's me cook with her. It is so much fun. I love licking the batter off of the spoon. Maybe when your mom has a few minutes, the two of you could make cupcakes. Oops, I almost forgot the best part: THEN YOU CAN EAT THEM!

2 1/4 cups of regular flour
1 1/3 cups sugar
3 teaspoons of baking powder
1 cup milk
I tablespoon vanilla
2 large eggs
1/2 cup shortening
A pinch of salt

Cupcakes

Mix it all together and pour into baking cups (1/2 full). Place in pre-heated oven (350) and cook for 17-25 minutes.

Do Not Touch The Stove Without Your Mommy or Daddy!

FLOWER

My flower has a face because I think flowers look happy even if they cannot smile. Flowers do make people smile though and they are special, just like you! Can you draw a flower right next to mine below? That way, my flower will have a friend just like us.

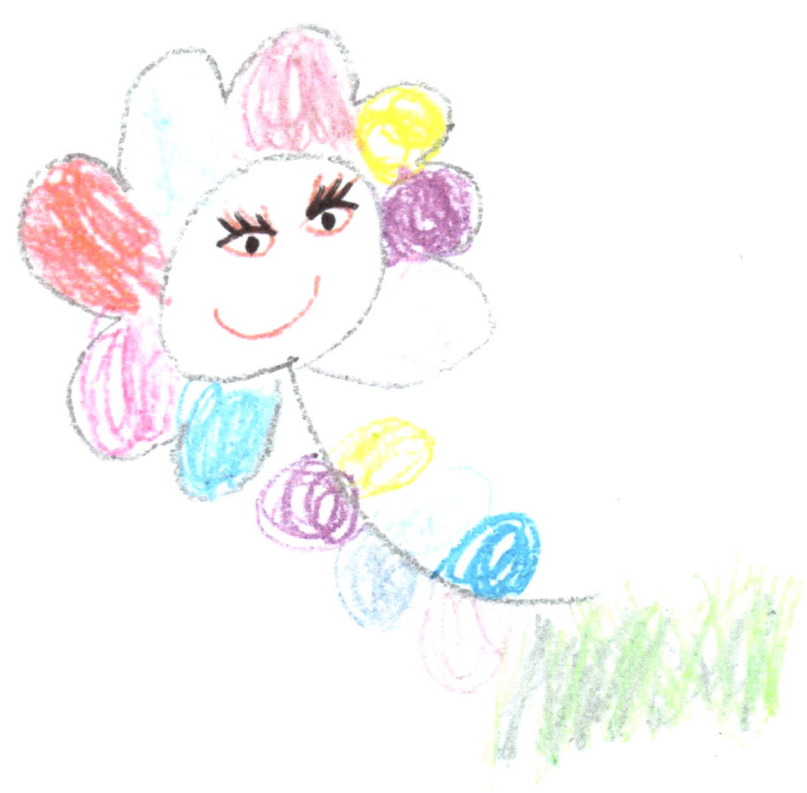

My picture needs more flowers, a sun, some grass and a bird. Can you draw them for me? Great!

TREE

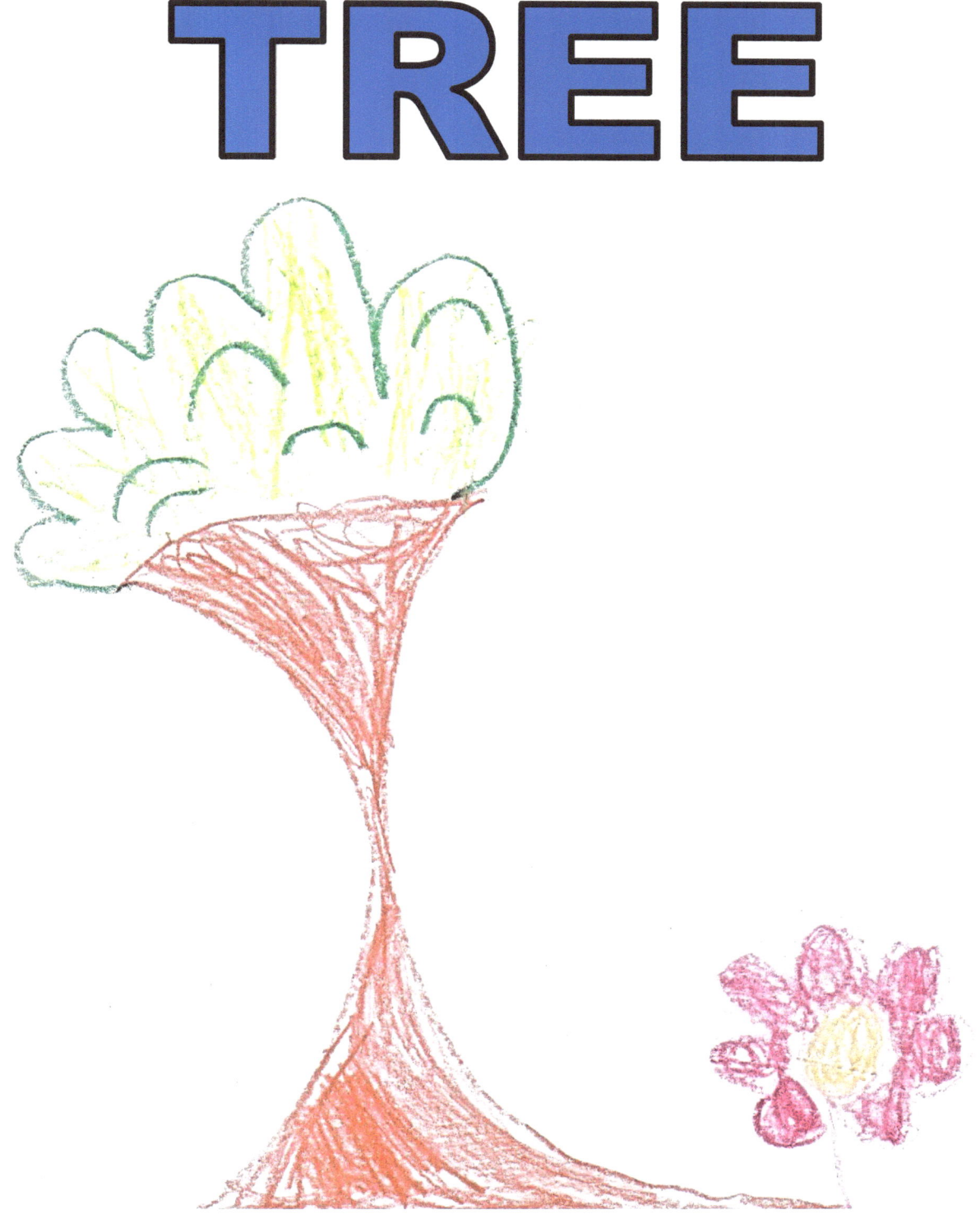

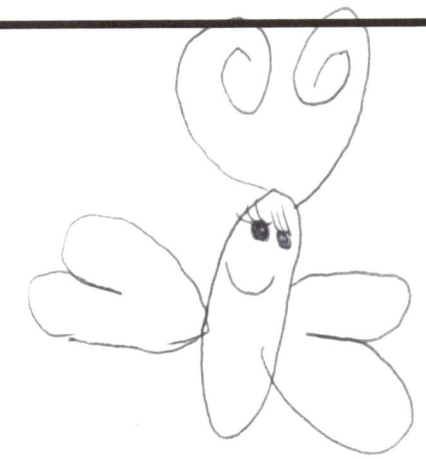

Color Me!

Can you color this picture for me? I think it also needs grass. What do you think?

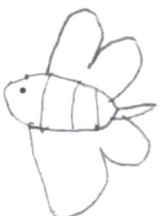

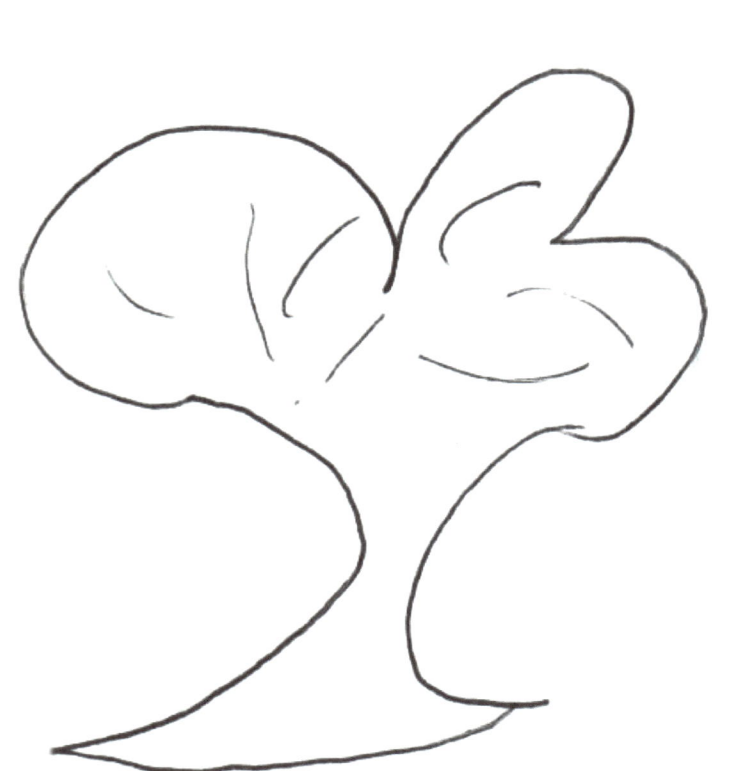

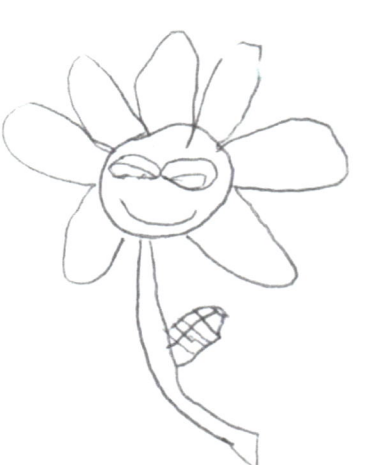

PINK

Could you ever imagine a
world without color?

I love colors and to color!

Can you draw something
in your favorite color?

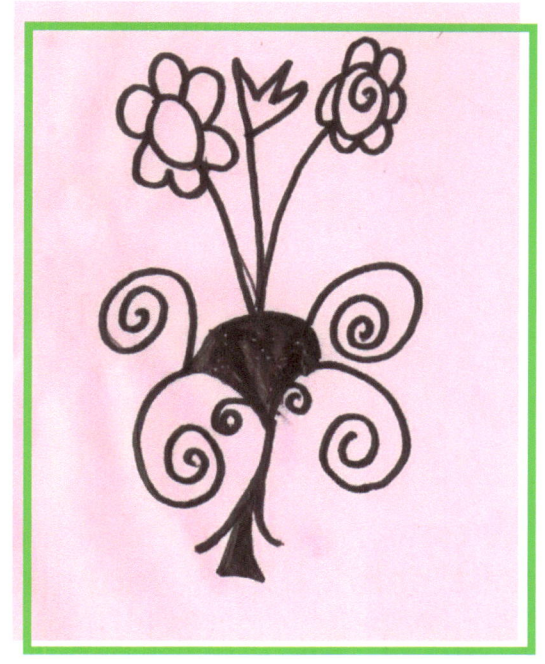

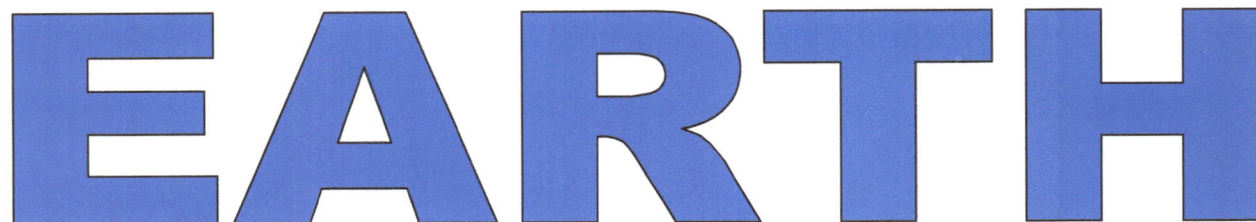

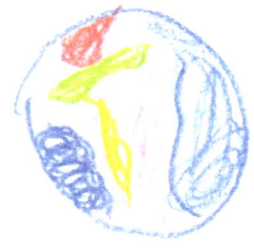

At school I am learning about the world. Wow, is it big! I surprised my Mommy and Daddy with this picture. Can you draw our earth? I can't wait to see it!

CHORES

I have chores to do every week at my house. Sometimes, I am a little messy and I do not put away my crayons and paper. My mommy will then ask me to clean my room. Yuck. But, after I clean it, I am happy that I did because my room looks so much better!

Sometimes if I help with my baby brothers stuff, Daddy gives me a dollar!

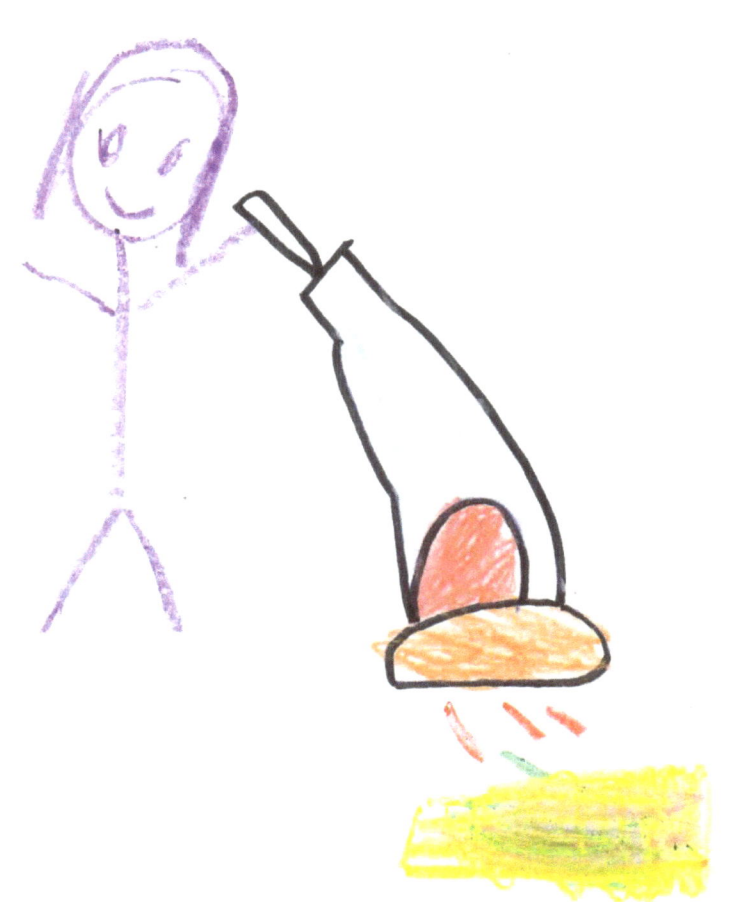

DRAW ANYTHING YOU WANT!

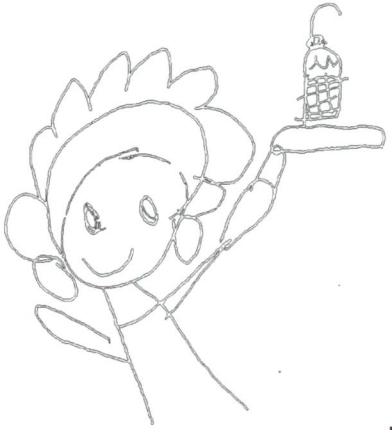

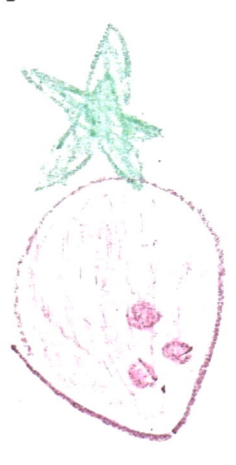

STRAWBERRY

DRAW ANYTHING YOU WANT!

Be Creative!

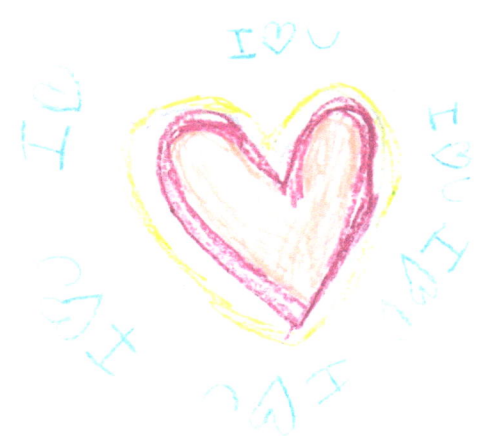

PUMPKIN

I love to put faces on pumpkins! Can you draw me a face? Before you start, think about what kind of face you want to draw. Will it be a scary one, happy one or funny one? Have fun!

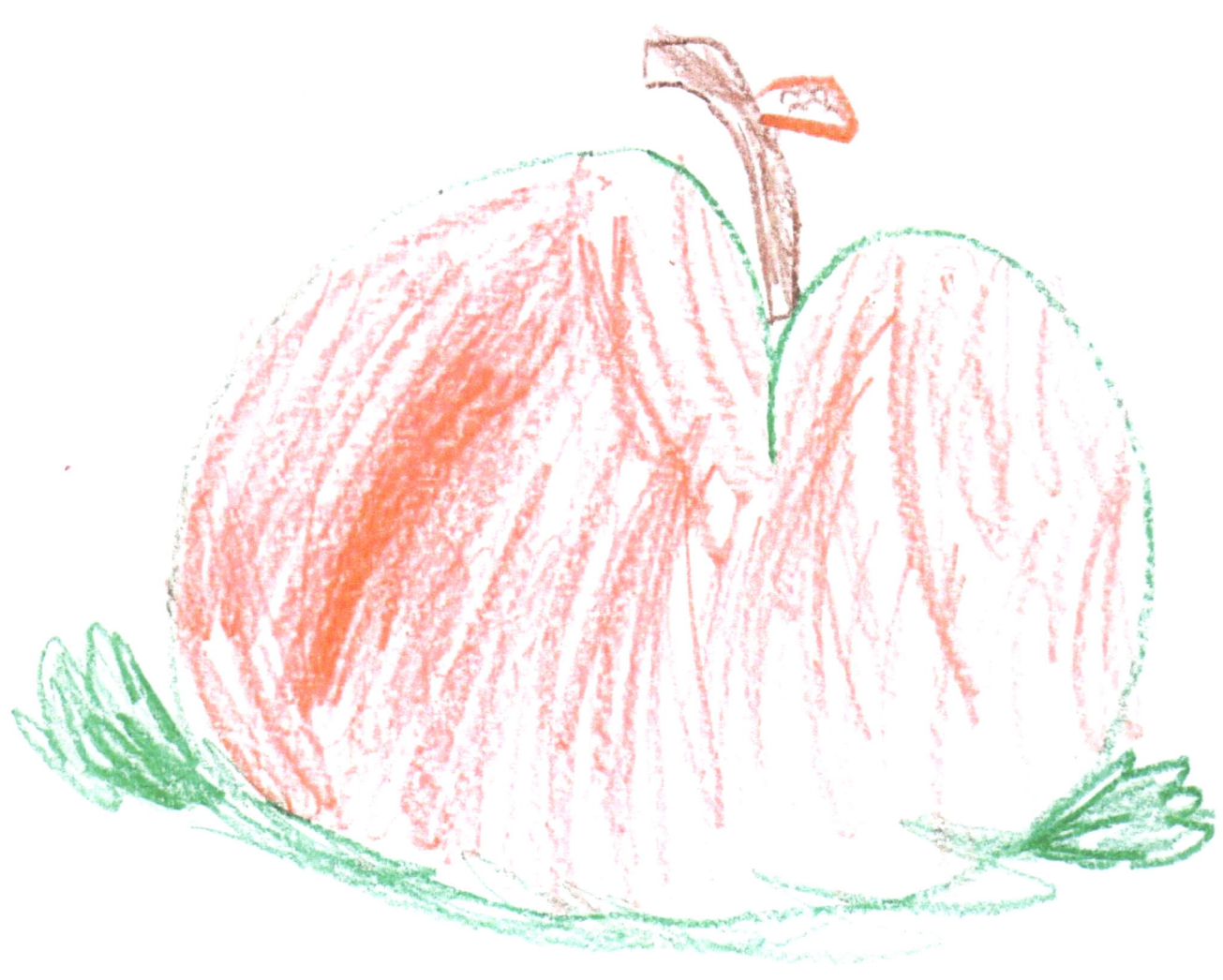

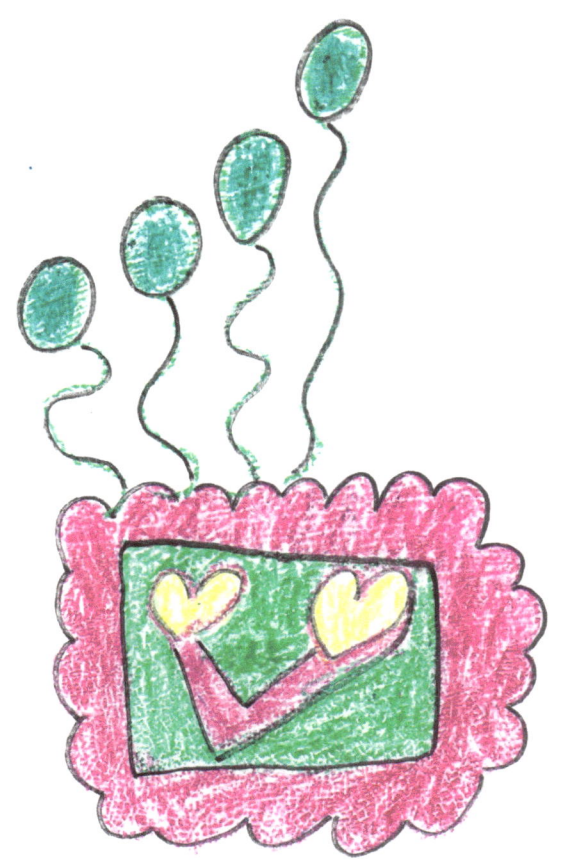

Make Your Design!

I like using colors!

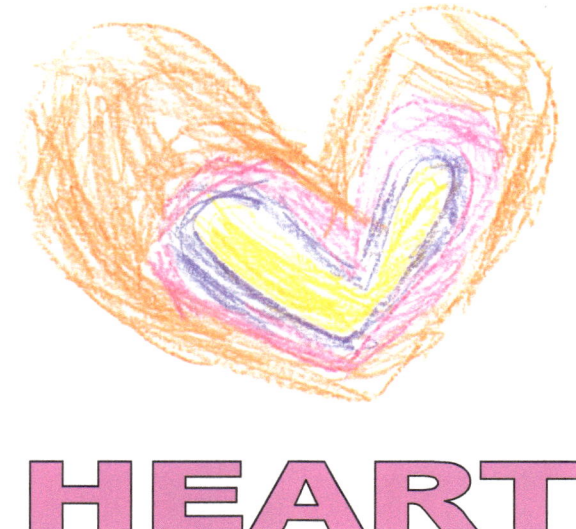

HEART

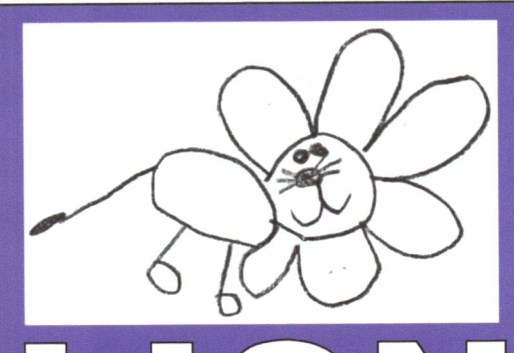

LION

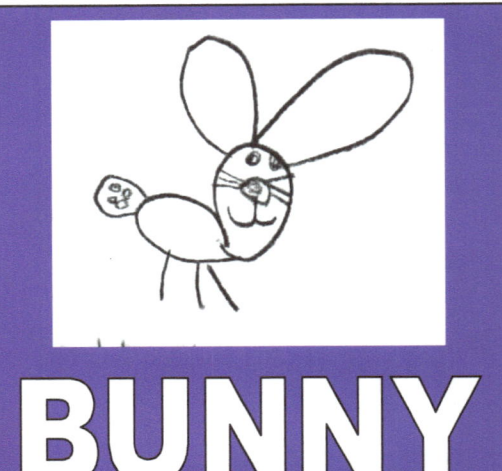

BUNNY

I think a couple of
my animals are miss-
ing their happy face.
Can you draw them
for me?

Super!

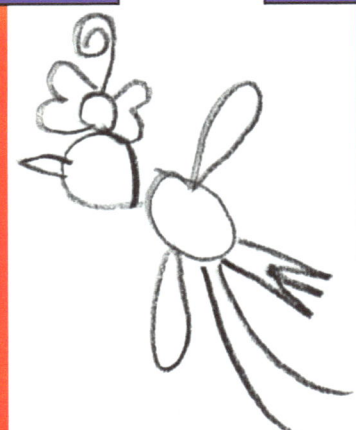

BIRD

Use A Pencil

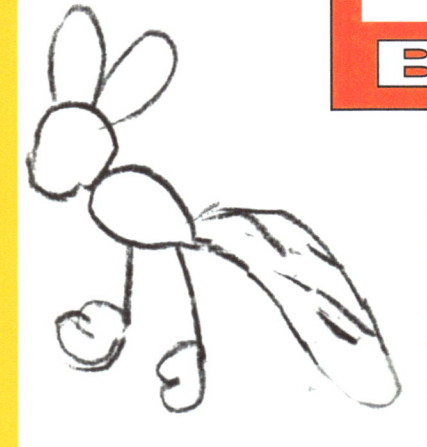

FOX

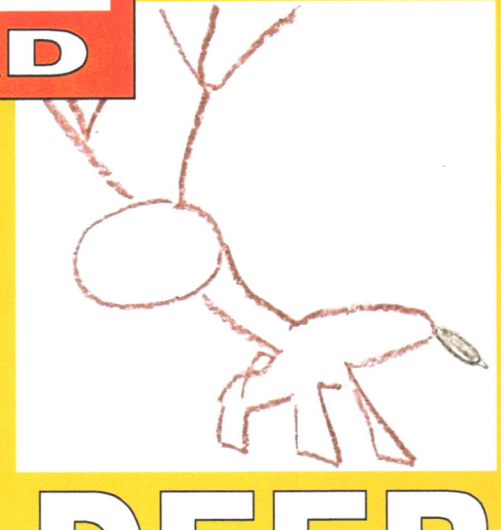

DEER

COW

Draw These Animals!

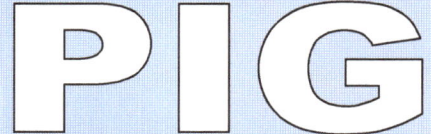

WITCH

Spooky!

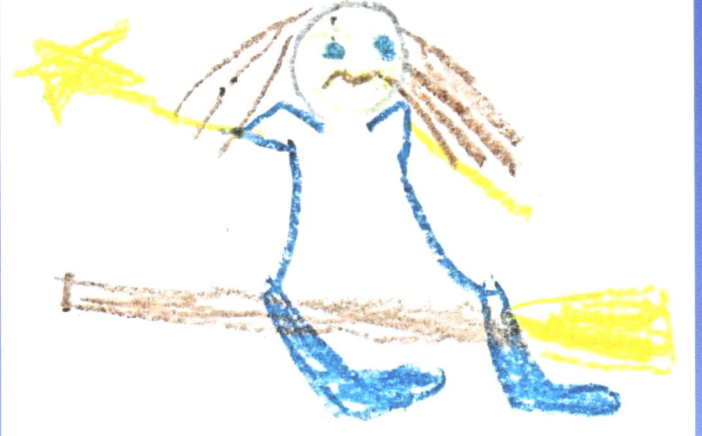

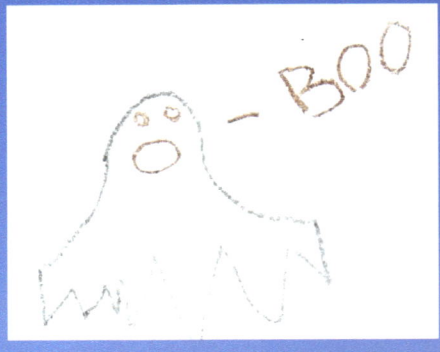

GHOST

CAN YOU DRAW ME A PICTURE?

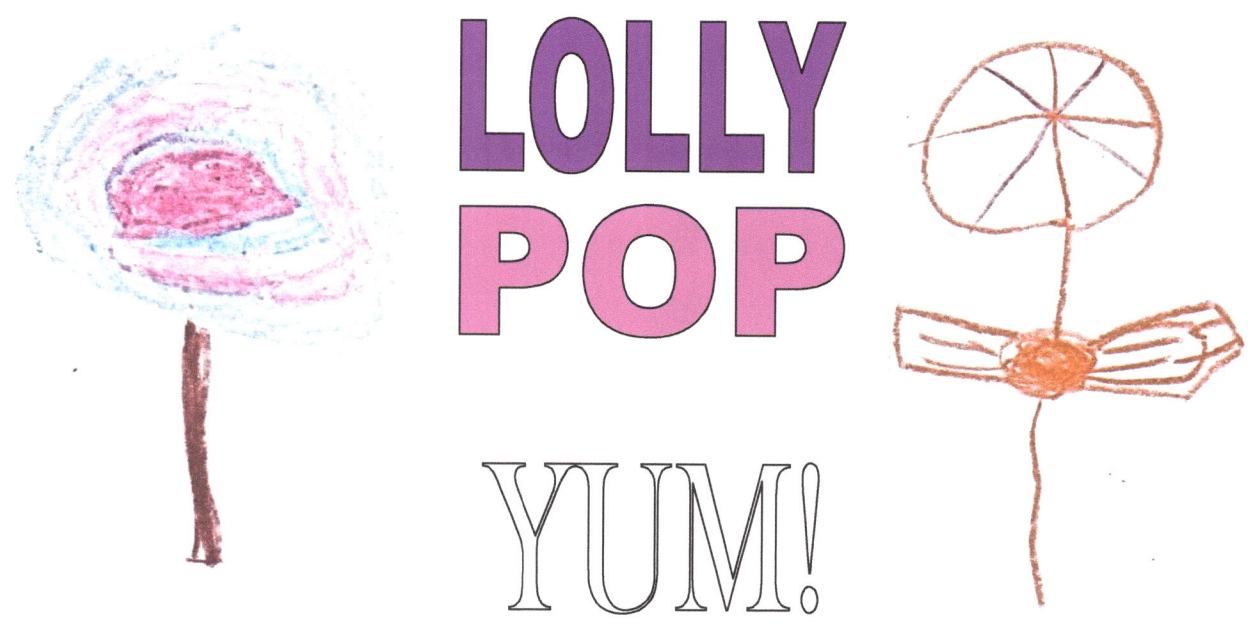

LOLLY
POP

YUM!

DRAW ME SOME CANDY!

A

B

B is for broccoli

A is for apple

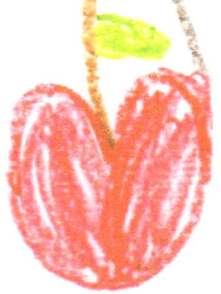

K

K is for corn— oops it should be....

I LOVE

LEARNING!

C is for corn
Can you fix my mistake?

Thank You For Drawing With Me!

I would love to stay friends with you and see your works of art. You can write to me at Bailey@sebipublishing.com with your parents permission and help. You can also have your parents email me copies of your artwork! I knew you had talent and creativity! **You are special, just like me!**

Remember that drawing is much more fun then watching tv or playing video games. Being creative exercises our brains!

Love,
Bailey de Cardenas

"Get Ready, Grab Your Crayons, Let's Go Draw!"

Use The Extra Pages To Make More Drawings!

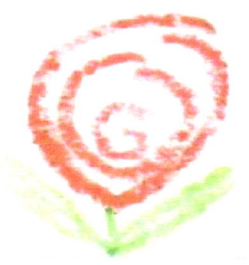

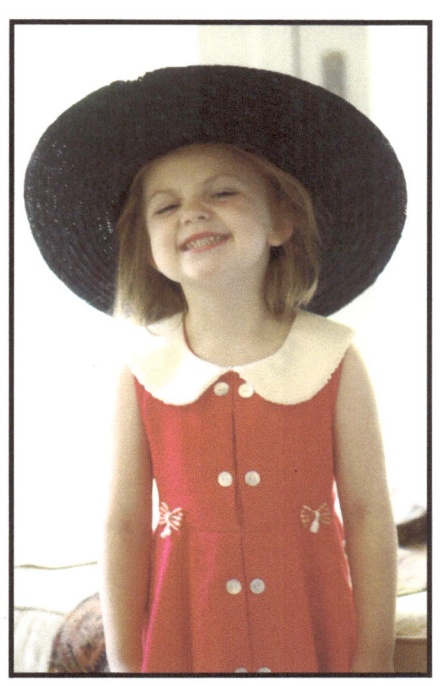

www.ingramcontent.com/pod-product-compliance
Lightning Source LLC
Chambersburg PA
CBHW050411180526
45159CB00005B/2232